If there's ever a time...to fill your bookshelves with information and grow as much food and herbs as possible ...it's now.

DELCI PLOUFFE

TABLE OF CONTENTS

I am not a trained vet! I have gathered this information through my own experiences and reading and education but always recommend you speak to a vet who understands goats before making final assessments of your herd.

STOCK UP

Most likely you can't grow these items.

- Cinnamon Powder
- Cloves/Clove Powder
- Gentian Root
- Ginger Powder
- Kelp
- Oak Bark
- Probios
- Seaweed Powder

- Slippery Elm Powder
- Spirulina Powder
- Tumeric Powder

ESSENTIAL OILS

HOME SUPPLIES

HERBS

HERBS

Plant as many herbs as you can that grow in your garden zone.
Then harvest, preserve, and use them each year.
After that, fill your pantry with herbs that you can NOT grow by
purchasing them from reputable companies and herbalists.

ESSENTIAL OILS

☐ Oregano Oil	☐ Eucalyptus Oil	☐ Rosemary Oil
☐ Peppermint Oil	☐ Citronella Oil	☐
☐ Tea Tree Oil	☐ Cedarwood Oil	☐
☐ Lavender Oil	☐ Lemongrass Oil	☐

HOME SUPPLIES

☐ Aloe Vera juice	☐ Corn Syrup	☐ Oats (oatmeal)
☐ Antacids	☐ Diatomaceous Earth DE	☐ Olive Oil
☐ Apple Cider Vinegar	☐ Ensure (or generic)	☐ Peanut Butter
☐ Aspirin	☐ Epsom Salts	☐ Powdered camphor
☐ Baking Soda	☐ Flaxseed oil	☐ Sea salt
☐ Bananas	☐ Flour	☐ Shea Butter
☐ Beeswax	☐ Honey	☐ Stout Beer
☐ Beer	☐ Karo Syrup	☐ Vodka/Brandy
☐ Benadryl	☐ Kefir	☐ Yogurt
☐ Bentonite Clay	☐ Linseed oil	☐
☐ Castile Soap	☐ Milk of Magnesia	☐
☐ Coconut Oil	☐ Molasses	☐
☐ Corn Oil	☐ Neem Oil	☐

GROWING LIST

HERBS

Grow as many as you can from the list below. For the ones that don't grow in your zone, add them to your shopping list to stock up on.

<table>
<tr><td>☐ Anise</td><td>☐ Mullein</td></tr>
<tr><td>☐ Astragalus</td><td>☐ Mustard</td></tr>
<tr><td>☐ Borage</td><td>☐ Nettle</td></tr>
<tr><td>☐ Burdock</td><td>☐ Oregano</td></tr>
<tr><td>☐ Chamomile</td><td>☐ Parsley</td></tr>
<tr><td>☐ Comfrey</td><td>☐ Peppermint</td></tr>
<tr><td>☐ Dandelion</td><td>☐ Plantain</td></tr>
<tr><td>☐ Dock</td><td>☐ Psyllium</td></tr>
<tr><td>☐ Elderberry</td><td>☐ Red Raspberry Leaf</td></tr>
<tr><td>☐ Fennel</td><td>☐ Rose Hips</td></tr>
<tr><td>☐ Fenugreek</td><td>☐ Rosemary</td></tr>
<tr><td>☐ Garlic</td><td>☐ Sage</td></tr>
<tr><td>☐ Ginger</td><td>☐ Southernwood (artemisia)</td></tr>
<tr><td>☐ Goldenseal</td><td>☐ Thyme</td></tr>
<tr><td>☐ Ivy</td><td>☐ Wild mustard</td></tr>
<tr><td>☐ Lemon Balm</td><td>☐ Wormwood</td></tr>
<tr><td>☐ Lobelia Inflata</td><td>☐ Yarrow</td></tr>
<tr><td>☐ Marshmallow Root</td><td>☐</td></tr>
<tr><td>☐</td><td>☐</td></tr>
<tr><td>☐</td><td>☐</td></tr>
<tr><td>☐</td><td>☐</td></tr>
<tr><td>☐</td><td>☐</td></tr>
</table>

GROWING LIST

GARDEN / CROPS

Grow as many as you can from the list below. For the ones that don't grow in your zone or you don't have the land to grow them on, add them to your shopping list to stock up on.

- [ ] Alfalfa
- [ ] Barley
- [ ] Beets
- [ ] Carrots
- [ ] Cayenne Peppers
- [ ] Corn
- [ ] Garlic
- [ ] Iodine rich foods
- [ ] Leafy/woody food
- [ ] Linseed/flaxseed
- [ ] Oats

- [ ] Plants rich in aromatic oils
- [ ] Pumpkins
- [ ] Red Clover
- [ ] Sweet Potatoes
- [ ] Wheat bran
- [ ]
- [ ]
- [ ]
- [ ]
- [ ]
- [ ]

GROWING LIST

FLOWER GARDEN/TREES

Grow as many as you can from the list below. For the ones that don't grow in your zone, add them to your shopping list to stock up on.

- [ ] Calendula
- [ ] Chamomile
- [ ] Echinacea
- [ ] Passion Flower
- [ ] Skullcap
- [ ] Sunflowers
- [ ]

- [ ] Black Walnut (Tree)
- [ ] Cloves (Tree)
- [ ] Eucalyptus (Tree)
- [ ] Oak (Tree)
- [ ] Slippery Elm (Tree)
- [ ]

HERBS

GARDEN / CROPS

FLOWER GARDEN

- [ ] https://mountainroseherbs.com
- [ ] https://www.starwest-botanicals.com/shop-by-category/
- [ ] https://drchristophersherbshop.com
- [ ] https://www.herbco.com
- [ ] https://leaves.shoplightspeed.com/products/
- [ ] https://www.revive-eo.com
- [ ] https://www.youngliving.com/us/en
- [ ] https://www.doterra.com/US/en
- [ ]
- [ ]

Definitions:

- **Infusion:** Tea made from leaves or flowers of an herb. Pour boiling water over plant parts and steep for 10-20 minutes. Use 1 tsp of dried herb or 3 tsp of fresh herb to 1 cup of boiling water. Can be drunk, used as a wash, soak, compress, or massaged into skin, or steam inhaled.
- **Decoction:** Made from tougher parts of plants like the seeds, roots, or bark. Simmer 1 tablespoon of chopped-up herb parts to 1-1.5 cups of water for 5-30 minutes.
- **Tincture:** Liquid form of herb that is very concentrated. Add 1-2 ounces of finely chopped or powdered herb to 1 quart of brandy, gin, or vodka and steep for several weeks or months. Administered by adding drops from an eye dropper to water and drinking. Can be stored unrefrigerated for up to 2 years.
- **Poultice/Plaster:** Mixture of herbs, either dried or fresh, moistened with water or oil, and applied to an area of concern. Applied hot, it's called a poultice, and applied cold it's called a plaster. Usually applied between pieces of fabric for protection of skin and easy cleanup.
- **Compress:** A cloth is dipped in liquid of an infusion, decoction, or water, either warm or room temperature.
- **Salves/Ointments:** Creams with 1 or more herbs heated in an oil. After the solids are strained out, beeswax is added to the warm oil to create a warm, easily spreadable cream.
- **Liniment:** Oil-based with no added beeswax. Usually, a heat-producing herb, like cayenne pepper or mustard is used and rubbed into the skin to increase blood flow.

anise | an ˌise | *noun*

Mediterranean plant of the parsley family, cultivated for its aromatic seeds which are used in cooking and herbal medicine.

A great option to relieve gas buildup, as in the case of colic. Helps with all digestive problems.
Dose*: One heaping handful of seeds daily on average.*

blackberry | blak-ˌber-ē | *noun*

the usually black or dark purple juicy but seedy edible aggregate fruit of various brambles (genus Rubus) of the rose family.

Very important plant eaten with voracity by all animals. Allow this to grow in as many areas as possible on your property.
Brew: *Roots is a great remedy for diarrhea because it's an astringent.*
Foliage: *Eczema.*
Tonic herb in pregnancy. Give leaves during periods of lack of appetite.
Dose: *2 handfuls of leaves and fruit daily.*
1 handful of leaves brewed in 1.5 pints of water. Clean affected area with brew several times a day.
Pluck a fresh leaf, heat over a fire, and lay the leaf on the affected area. The underside will draw out and the top side will soothe.

black walnut hull | blæk ˌwɔlħət | *noun*

a walnut of eastern North America with hard strong heavy dark brown wood and oily edible nuts.

Take great care in feeding black walnuts to pregnant goats.
This can be turned into a salve or a tincture.
**Prolonged use is not advised due to the presence of significant quantities of juglone, a known mutagen in animals.*

borage | bȯr-ij | *noun*

a hardy, annual, prickly, European herb with star-shaped blue flowers that is widely naturalized as a weed and has leaves used as remedies in herbal medicine and also as food, especially in salads.

Great for heart and chest issues, including coughs, and rickets, and is a mild laxative.
Touted to increase milk flow.
It can be used as an eye lotion and a ringworm remedy.
Dose: *2-4 handfuls mixed with grain, one or two times daily.*
Lotion: *1 handful to 1/2 pint water.*

HERBS

burdock root | bər-ˌdäk ṙüt | *noun*

any of a genus of coarse herbs that are related to the daisies and have globe-shaped flower heads surrounded by prickly bracts.

One of the best blood cleansers. Aids in cough and skin parasites.
Leaves: *bruised, applied externally, remedy for ringworm and scabies.*
Fruits & Roots: *make excellent lotion for burn treatments.*
Dose: *brew 2 ounces of sliced root in two pints of water. Give half a pint morning and night on an empty stomach.*
Can be infused into oils for salves, burn washes, and abscess cleansers.

cayenne | ˌkī(y)en, ˌkā(y)en | *noun*

a pungent hot-tasting red powder prepared from ground dried chili peppers.

Increases body temperature, metabolism and normalizes glucose lives. Contains many B vitamins, has great antiseptic properties, stops blood flow in an external wound and with internal hemorrhaging. It also invigorates weak animals.
Goat Kids: *pinch of powder rubbed on gums or dip finger in honey and then dip in cayenne and rub on gums.*
Adult Goats: *Good-sized pinch rubbed on gums or dip 2 fingertips with honey and dip in cayenne*
Do this every 15 minutes until temperatures return to normal.

calendula | kə-len-jə-lə | *noun*

Any of numerous chiefly annual herbs of the genus Calendula widely cultivated for their yellow or orange flowers; often used for medicinal and culinary purposes.

Also known as pot marigold, is mostly used as a topical anti-inflammatory and antiseptic. Make salves and infused oils.

chamomile | kaməˌmēl,kaməˌmīl | *noun*

Chamomile is a plant with pretty little white flowers and a sweet smell. Dried chamomile is often used to make herbal tea.

May increase milk yield and butterfat content in goat's milk. And may soothe the stomach. Helps aid in the reduction of pain, and inflammation.
Dose: *Brew 1 handful of flowers in 2 pints of water. Add 1 tablespoon of honey. Drink 2 times a day, morning and evening.*

Timing of Harvest:
1. **Roots:** Collect in fall
2. **Bark from Trees:** Picked in late winter/early spring
3. **Leaves/Stems:** Collect just before the plant begins to bloom
4. **Flowers:** Take when first open
5. **Seeds:** When they just reach maturity.

chives | CHīvz | *noun*

a widely cultivated small Eurasian plant related to the onion, with purple-pink flowers and dense tufts of long tubular leaves that are used as a culinary herb.

Animals love this plant and instinctively know that it is a tonic and internally cleansing and aids in worm removal.
Dose: *Handful daily in bran mash.*

cinnamon | ṡinəmən | *noun*

An aromatic spice made from the peeled, dried, and rolled bark of a Southeast Asian tree.

Kills cocci, and can stop scours and diarrhea. Full of nutrients!
Goat Kids *(up to 3 months): 1/4-1/2 tsp daily.*
Adult Goats: *1-2 tsp or up to 1 tbsp every 1-2 hours.*

clover | klōvər | *noun*

a herbaceous plant of the pea family that has dense, globular flower heads, and leaves that are typically three-lobed. It is an important and widely grown fodder and rotational crop.

This is a wonderful crop to plant and is known for its ability to provide a superb food value and the flowers are known to help with infertility, coughs, and nerves.

comfrey | kəmfrē | *noun*

(plural comfreys) a Eurasian plant of the borage family, with large hairy leaves and clusters of purplish or white bell-shaped flowers.

Supports bone healing after a break or fracture. Aids in stopping internal hemorrhaging. Helps with bad bruises, swelling, and sprains. Leaves are used for external use only. See recipes in this book. Once established, separate patch by division to expand.

crab apple | krab ˌapəl | *noun*

a small sour apple.

The crab apple releases its nutrients immediately making it superb for stomach and intestinal and diarrhea issues. It's also a great nerve and heart tonic.
Feed a cup before evening meals.

Ironically, poor soil quality will produce an herb that has the most aromatic foliage while fertile soil will produce an herb with more leaves but less aroma.

currant | kərənt | *noun*

the acid-edible fruit of various shrubs (genus Ribes) placed in either the saxifrage or gooseberry family.

The black currant is considered anti-abortive and will help with pregnancy weakness, anemia, and bladder issues and is helpful in fevers.
Dose*: feed handfuls of the herb, both the foliage and twigs, daily, mixed with grain. You can also give 2 tablespoons of puree or 4 tablespoons of crushed raw berries 2 times a day. For fevers, give 1 cupful of crushed berries twice a day.*

dandelion root | dandlˌīən,dandēˌlīən | *noun*

a widely distributed weed of the daisy family, with a rosette of leaves, bright yellow flowers followed by globular heads of seeds with downy tufts, and stems containing a milky latex.

Considered a terrible weed by most, it is one of the most valuable among herbalists. Blood cleansing, the leaves strengthen the enamel of the teeth and the white juice dissolves warts.
Dose: *5 raw roots or a handful of leaves daily.*

dill | dil/ | *noun*

an aromatic annual herb of the parsley family, with fine blue-green leaves and yellow flowers. The leaves and seeds of dill are used for flavoring and medicinal purposes.

The seed of the dill plant is used. It is known to increase milk yield. Will also help with digestive issues, diarrhea, and fever. Grows tall, plant at the back of the garden.
Dose*: Handful of seed mixed with grain, up to two times a day.*

dock | däk | *noun*

rumex bucephalophorus (Red Dock) is a species of annual herb in the family Polygonaceae. They have a self-supporting growth form. They have simple, broad leaves and achenes.

Cooling herb, helping hot and inflamed skin, including mastitis. The entire herb, both the leaves and roots is an antiseptic.
Add one handful of cut leaves to 1.5 pints of water for a brew. Pulp the leaves, warm over a fire, and place on inflamed skin.

Dry any plant thoroughly to prevent mold!
Annuals: harvest the entire plant.
Perennials: pick 1/3 of the plant and allow enough time for regrowth before winter arrives.

echinacea | e-ki-ḣā-sē-ə | *noun*

a North American coneflower. It is used in herbal medicine, largely for its antibiotic and wound-healing properties.

The dried rhizome, roots, or other parts of any of the three purple coneflowers are used primarily in dietary supplements and herbal remedies for the stimulating effect they are held to have on the immune system. Find recipes in this book for use. An infusion can be made out of the leaves and petals. Grow from seed or from division.

elderberry | ėldər͵berē | *noun*

the bluish-black or red berry of the elder, used especially for making jelly or wine. an elder tree or shrub.

Blossom: most potent for internal use. Used in lotion for treatment of skin issues (brew in water or buttermilk).
Foliage: external treatments.
Berry juice: excellent for coughs. Mix with egg white for an effective salve for burns and scalds.
Roots: a brew made with finely shaved roots is great for kidney problems and dropsy.
Internal dose: Add 1 handful of cut leaves or blossom to 1/5 pints of water, and add 2 spoonfuls of honey or molasses. Give one cupful morning and evening.
External dose: Leave out honey or molasses, and add more herbs to make it more potent.
Berries dose: heat slightly and pound

fennel | fen(ə)l | *noun*

an aromatic yellow-flowered European plant of the parsley family, with feathery leaves.

Many claim that this herb will increase milk and give the milk a sweet smell. It can be used both internally and externally. The seeds produce a sweet oil that has high medicinal value. It can be used for colic, inflammation of the bowels, and constipation. Also for fevers, cramps; and worms and as an eye ointment.

fenugreek | fen(y)ə͵grēk | *noun*

a white-flowered herbaceous plant of the pea family, with aromatic seeds that are used for flavoring, especially ground and used in curry powder.

Seeds: highly aromatic, powerful disinfectant and lubricant properties.
This herb is fattening, helps increase milk supply, and is rich in vitamins, which will enhance fertility.
Dose: 2 handfuls of plant-fed daily. Or use the seed and feed 2 ounces of seed daily. The seed can be used for making a poultice.
An external poultice can relieve abscesses, boils, and sores.

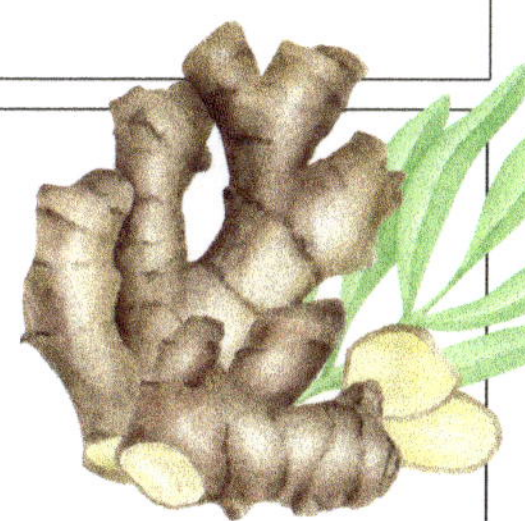

garlic | ġärlik | *noun*

a white-flowered herbaceous plant of the pea family, with aromatic seeds that are used for flavoring, especially ground and used in curry powder.

One clove a day keeps mastitis at bay! Helps heal respiratory illness and open sores. Repels ticks and prevents parasites. Destroys bacteria, and fungi. Always have it on hand. Studies show that bacteria don't evolve into resistance like with antibiotic medications.
Feed raw cloves 3-4 times a week.
Illness: recipes found in this book.

ginger | jinjər | *noun*

a hot, fragrant spice made from the rhizome of a plant, which may be chopped or powdered for cooking, preserved in syrup, or candied.

Ginger has antioxidant properties, anti-bacterial action, and anti-inflammatory effects. Find recipes in this book.

goldenseal | gōldənˌsēl | *noun*

a North American woodland plant of the buttercup family, with a bright yellow root that is used in herbal medicine.

The respiratory tract, gastrointestinal tract, lower urinary tract, eyes, and mouth all can find beneficial uses for goldenseal. The indigenous peoples of North America have traditionally used it as an insect deterrent and ointment for wounds, ulcers, and inflamed eyes. The herb was used internally to treat liver and stomach issues. Antibiotic, anti-inflammatory, astringent, disinfectant, anti-catarrhal, antibacterial, anti-fungal, anti-parasitic, and immuno-stimulating.

ivy | īvē/ | *noun*

a woody evergreen Eurasian climbing plant, typically having shiny, dark green five-pointed leaves.

Very useful in a poultice, when it's combined with other herbs. The ivy draws out the medicinal properties of the other herbs.
Dose: *2 Tablespoons of fresh leaves in a bran mash. Or brew 1 handful in 1.5 cups water and add honey. Give three times a day.*
Poultice: *ivy, ragwort, and groundsel in equal parts--treats skin and tumors.*
ivy, yarrow, and chamomile--treats skin diseases, abscesses, and boils.
Ivy, licorice, and honey--pulmonary ailments and tuberculosis.

HERBS

lemon balm | lɛmən bɑːm | *noun*

lemon balm is a perennial herbaceous plant in the mint family and native to south-central Europe, the Mediterranean Basin, Iran, and Central Asia, but now naturalized elsewhere. It grows to a maximum height of 1 m. The leaves have a mild lemon scent. During summer, small white flowers full of nectar appear.

Lemon Balm is a relaxing herb, along with calming the stomach. It is highly flavorful and packed with nutrients. Anti-viral, anti-depressant, anxiety, insomnia, headaches, colds and flu, menstrual cramps, digestive aid, intestinal spasms, gas.

lobelia Inflata | lō-bēl-yə | *noun*

Carrier herb.

This is a very important herb to an herbalist. Add it to any herbal mix and it will guide the other herbs to get where they need to be to work properly.
Can work with mullein to help with glandular issues.
Also known as Indian Tobacco.
***Dose:** Brew 2 handfuls of the herb in 1.5 pints of water, add two spoonfuls of honey. Give 2 cupfuls two times a day.*
Make a poultice or brew for external use.
Boil 4-6 sliced roots for 2 hours in one quart of water, give half a pint twice daily.

marshmallow root | ṁärsh-ˌme-lō , ṙüt | *noun*

Althaea officinalis

Used to soothe irritation in the stomach or stop scouring and diarrhea and can reduce swelling. It is also helpful for sore and inflamed udders.
***Dose:** Boil 3-4 sliced roots for one hour in 2 pints of water. Add honey, raisins, and 6 cloves. Give this 3 times daily.*
Pulped leaves and blossoms, slightly heated, are excellent for a lotion for external injuries.
Fresh and dried roots are very nutritious and soothing and are great for young and sick animals.

mullein | ṁəl(ə)n | *noun*

many useful uses including treatment for cough, bronchitis, tuberculosis, asthma, and pneumonia. Also good for diarrhea and internal bleeding.

Store flowers out of light because they turn black in light. Seeds are toxic.
***Uses:** Powdered roots fatten poultry.*
Another name for mullein is candlewick because the down from the soft leaves can be scraped off, compressed, and used as wicks in candles.
***Dose:** Brew a handful in 1.5 pints of water and give it morning and night. Can also be used in a poultice recipe.*

mustard | ˈməstərd | *noun*

the mustard plant is any one of several plant species in the genera Brassica, Rhamphospermum, and Sinapis in the family Brassicaceae (the mustard family).

Rich in antioxidants and antibiotic properties and has disinfectant properties. It promotes appetite and the seeds are a worm-repellent and when chewed will help toothaches.
Oil form: *without proper dilution, will cause burns and blisters. 2 ml olive oil per drop of essential oil for oral use. Not safe for use in pregnancy.*
Coccidiosis*: shown to both treat and prevent.*
Dose*: 4 handfuls of the whole plant and 2 handfuls of the seed added to a bran mash. 2 spoonfuls of molasses can be added and given twice daily. Externally, a poultice or lotion can be made with mustard flour.*

nasturtium | ˈhastərSH(ə)m | *noun*

a South American trailing plant with round leaves and bright orange, yellow, or red edible flowers that is widely grown as an ornamental.

Animals love this plant and it is very nutritious, a strong antiseptic, cleansing, and a vermifuge, the seeds especially. The seeds can be placed in vinegar to make a tonic and anti-worm remedy. This is also a fertility herb.
Dose: *Feed several handfuls of leaves daily. And to treat worms, one spoonful of seeds.*

nettle | ned(ə)l | *noun*

a herbaceous plant which has jagged leaves covered with stinging hairs.

Rich source of chlorophyll. Rich in minerals: iron, lime, sodium, chlorine, and a lot of protein! Prevents worms and increases milk yield.
(Poultry fattener: cut up young leaves and give raw. Boil older leaves and mash in with feed.)
Nettle juice mixed with nettle seed is great to rinse hair in (your own!) and nettle will give animals a shine to their coat!

oregano | ˈə-ˈre-gə-ˌnō | *noun*

an aromatic plant related to marjoram, with leaves that are used fresh or dried as a culinary herb.

Rich in antioxidants and antibiotic properties.
Oil form: *without proper dilution, will cause burns and blisters. 2 ml olive oil per drop of essential oil for oral use. This oil is powerful and must be used with discretion and wisdom. Only use at weaning to prevent coccidiosis.*
Give dried or fresh.

parsley | pärslē | *noun*

a biennial plant with white flowers and aromatic leaves that are either crinkly or flat and used as a culinary herb and for garnishing food.

This is a great herb to grow. Goats love it and all of the plant can be used. It will increase milk yield. And is very high in iron and copper.
Dose: *Give 3 handfuls fed 2 times a day, or 3 roots daily, or 2 ounces of seed daily. Fresh leaves, steeped in vinegar, are great for soothing stings.*

peppermint | ˌpepərˌmint | *noun*

the aromatic leaves of a plant of the mint family, or an essential oil obtained from them, used as a flavoring in food.

This very aromatic plant can be cut up by a handful daily and added to the grain mix. The oil can be used in this manner: 6 drops, sprinkled and spread out on lumps of sugar or carrot slices.

plantain | plant(ə)n | *noun*

a low-growing plant that typically has a rosette of leaves and a slender green flower spike, widely growing as a weed in lawns, but is an important herb.

Goats love this plant and chickens love the seeds. The leaves make a wonderful healing ointment. It is very helpful to soothe bites and stings. And the root brew will help bring down a fever. Brew 2 handfuls of leaves brewed in 2 pints water--give 1 cupful 3 times a day.

psyllium | ˌsilēəm | *noun*

a leafy-stemmed Eurasian plantain, the seeds of which are used as a laxative.

Psyllium is a natural laxative, which can aid an herbal wormer in expelling worms.

red raspberry leaf | red ˌ ˌraz-ˌber-ē ˌ lēf | *noun*

the red raspberry leaf (Rubus idaeus), also known as garden raspberry leaf, is produced by the deciduous raspberry plant and used in folk remedies.

Promotes female health in goats and is said to cure sterility. Nourishing to sick or stressed goats. Use 3 parts raspberry leaf to one part feverfew to make a potent recipe for female use.
Dose: *2 handfuls given daily throughout the later half of pregnancy. Give a strong brew made of 2 handfuls of leaves, 1 pint of water, and 1 tablespoon of honey--give this frequently to bring down retained afterbirth. This same brew will help with diarrhea.*

rose hips | rōz ˌhɪp | *noun*

the fruit of a rose, especially a wild kind: the hips and haws in the hedges.

Best plant-derived source of Vitamin- C.
Dose: *2 handfuls of rose flowers once a day--can be pounded into 2 tablespoonfuls of honey. 15-20 rose hips daily, sliced, fed with grain.*

rosemary leaf | ŕōz-ˌmer-ē lēf | *noun*

an evergreen aromatic shrub of the mint family, native to southern Europe. The narrow leaves are used as a culinary herb, in perfumery, and as an emblem of remembrance.

This is a very important herb being an antiseptic and insecticide. Goats and sheep love to eat it and it gives a nice fragrance and tonic to their milk. Grows tall, plant at the back of the garden area.
Dose: *Give 3 handfuls, finely cut with grain, daily. Molasses can be added with a mash of bran. A strong brew or infused with oil is a good insecticide.*

sage | sāj | *noun*

an aromatic plant with grayish-green, fuzzy leaves that are used as a culinary herb, native to southern Europe and the Mediterranean.

Animals love sage. It makes milk refreshing and a tonic and will also increase milk yield. It is good for health both internally and externally. Grown in and among vegetable crops and vines, will give protection from insects and mice. It is also a fertility herb.
Dose: *Make a strong tea with 1 teaspoon of the herb to 2 cups of water. Or add 2 handfuls of the herb finely cut, into grain or mash daily, molasses can be added. For external use, brew one big handful in 1.5 pints of water.*

skullcap | ṡkəlˌkap | *noun*

derives its name from the caplike appearance of the outer whorl of its small blue or purple flowers. It is a slender, heavily-branched plant that grows to a height of 2 to 4 feet and blooms each July. It grows wild in woods and meadows.

Skullcap will help relax a nervous goat. An old cure for rabies. It will also help with a lack of appetite.
Dose: *Brew 1 handful of leaves in 1/5 pints of water, add 1 tablespoon of honey. Give one cupful three times a day. Find recipes in this book for the use of this dried herb.*

Research any medicinal herb before using it. Cross-reference and study herbs before moving forward with recipes. Seek professional advice if still unsure. Invest in "Peterson Field Guide to Medicinal Plants" for a go-to guide as you grow, harvest, and forage for medicinal herbs.

slippery elm | s̆lip(ə)rē elm | *noun*

a tree that is native to North America. Its inner bark feels slippery when chewed and may be effective for soothing sore throat. Only the inner bark of slippery elm, not the whole bark, is used as medicine.

The powdered bark has supreme healing properties.
Dose: Mix 2 tablespoons of elm powder into a tablespoon of honey and mix until smooth in texture, slowly stir in one pint of warm milk--give 1 cupful 2 times a day. The powder can be added to grain or bran gruel. Poultice: put some powdered elm in a flannel patch, fold it up, and place it in boiling water for 5 minutes--place over the affected area. See the poultice recipe in this book.

southernwood | s̆əTHərn͵wo͝od | *noun*

a bushy artemisia native to southern Europe.

Great help in birthing issues--see recipe. It is helpful to get rid of skin parasites and is a hair tonic. It has an essential oil, absinthol, which is said to be a worm excellent, antiseptic, tonic, and insect repellant.
Dose: Brew 1 handful of the herb in 2 pints of water, add 1 tablespoon of honey, and give morning and evening. Externally: use crushed leaves or the brew without the honey.

sunflowers | s̆ən͵flouər | *noun*

a tall North American plant of the daisy family, with very large golden-rayed flowers. Sunflowers are cultivated for their edible seeds.

Black oil sunflower seeds can be helpful for a doe that is in milk and need to gain weight. Do not give to bucks or wethers unless you have balanced their phosphorus-to-calcium ratio. These seeds are very high in fat but should not be given in excess.
Dose: Start by feeding 1/4 cup a day for a week. For hair shine and general health, feed 1/4-1/2 cup a day. For does that need extra weight feed up to 1 cup a day but. no more.

thyme | tīm | *noun*

a low-growing aromatic plant of the mint family. The small leaves are used as a culinary herb and the plant yields a medicinal oil.

The whole herb is highly tonic and antiseptic, the oil is even a worm expeller. Goats and sheep love to eat it because it's a milk tonic for them.
Dose: Brew one handful of finely cut leaves and mix in with their food and give one cupful 2 times a day.
An infusion in vinegar can be made to keep away biting insects.

When foraging wild edibles and medicinal plants, never pick the area clean. Always leave plant material behind so the plant can continue to grow and rejuvenate.

vetch | veCH | *noun*

a widely distributed scrambling herbaceous plant of the pea family, which is cultivated as a silage or fodder crop.

This is usually grown with rye, it provides valuable fodder, rich in nitrates and vitamins.

wormwood | wərmˌho͝od | *noun*

a woody shrub with a bitter aromatic taste used as an ingredient of vermouth and absinthe and in medicine.

It is famed as a worm remedy and aids in difficult births. Can be given a brew with sage and honey water.

Dose: *Brew 1 handful in 1.5 pints water and add 1 tablespoonful of honey, give 1 cupful 2 times a day.*

Care must be given with pregnant goats. In large quantities, it can cause problems. Do not use this during pregnancy until you are familiar with its uses and function and can dose properly.

yarrow | yerō | *noun*

a Eurasian plant of the daisy family, with feathery leaves and heads of small white, yellow, or pink aromatic flowers.

This is a wound herb and will help reduce fevers and help with pneumonia.
Do not use if on blood thinners.
Dose: *Give 2 handfuls of the herb, raw and finely cut. Brew 2 handfuls in 1.5 pints of water and give 2 cups morning and night. Use crushed and gently warmed leaves for earaches.*
A stronger brew can be made for external use by brewing 3 handfuls in 1.5 pints of water.

Herb Growing Tips

- **Plant according to height so the taller herbs don't shade the smaller herbs.**
- **It's best to begin by buying mint from a nursery. Because different types of mint cross with each other easily, their seed will not be true to flavor or type. After the mint is established, it can be propagated using cuttings from established plants.**
- **Mint can also become invasive. Plant in an area that you don't mind being overrun or plant in a container.**
- **Many herbs can be added to your garden by division or cuttings. Find a gardener in your area and ask if you can visit in the fall and divide up the parent plant. Dig up the parent plant, divide the roots into several pieces, and replant in your garden.**
- **Herbs that grow very well from cuttings: Lavender, mint, sage, thyme, and oregano. Mint and sage will grow roots very easily after placing 3-6 inches of green stem into a glass of water. Cut off any leaves that would be in the water. Otherwise, select 3-6 inches of green stem, dip in rooting hormone powder, and stick end in potting soil. Cover with a plastic bag and keep out of direct sunlight. Keep moist and open the bag periodically. Several weeks later growth will begin to appear.**

BEYOND HERBS

apple cidar vinegar

Added to water, ACV can be beneficial for health and can enhance the alkaline levels of the gut which can make it an unwelcome place for worms.
It's said to help create shiny hair coats, prevent mastitis, and increase milk production

Dose: Apple Cider Vinegar:
1 tablespoon to 1 gallon water.

baking soda

Baking soda can help when treating bloat.
There is controversy about feeding it free choice. Some claim that it has saved their goats from bloat because they self-medicate and others claim that free-choice baking soda causes their goats to stop creating their own and then without the baking soda they will bloat easier.

cob webs

Cobwebs can be used to stop bleeding. In ancient times, a combination of apple cider vinegar and honey would be used to clean the wounds and then the wound would be covered with balled-up spider webs.
They are also full of Vitamin K, which naturally helps with blood clotting and they are also a natural antiseptic and anti-fungal which keeps the wound clean and free from infections.

iodine

Can be used as an udder wash and is a great disinfectant. It is useful in destroying a wide range of pathogens harmful to goats such as viruses, bacteria, and fungi.

salt

Salt can be used to deter slugs and bugs from your herbs. It can also be used to cure animal hides.
Studies have shown: soaking 7% of table salt concentration can significantly accelerate the wound healing process compared to the control group, with a decrease in wound diameter on the 3rd day and completely heal on the 7th day.

karo syrup

Helpful in treating ketosis. Can be used in place of Nutri-Drench or propylene glycol for calorie boosts to does or kids with low energy.

sugar

Sugar can be used in the case of the prolapse. The prolapse would be rinsed and cleaned very well, sugar would be applied liberally and then the prolapse pushed back in. Many times in this case the goat needs a dose of calcium, possibly stitched up to hold in the prolapse and a vet to help.

PERENNIAL HERBS BY ZONE

Not all herbs will be used for goat care. But planting herbs for personal use, and also for bees, soil health, and companion planting will make you and your garden full of life. Double-check zone and planting information before planting herbs.

ZONE 3

Agrimony
Caraway
Catnip
Chamomile
Chives
Comfrey
Dog rose
Echinacea
Garlic
Garden sorrel
Hops
Horseradish
Parsley
Peppermint
Marshmallow
Spearmint

ZONE 4

Angelica
Anise
Catnip
Chives
Comfrey
Echinacea
Gentian
Hyssop
Lemon Balm
Marjoram
Marshmallow
Mint
Sage-Clary
Skullcap
St. John's Wort
Tarragon
Thyme
Valerian

ZONE 5

Angelica
Anise
Catnip
Chamomile
Chives
Comfrey
Echinacea
Feverfew
Gentian
Hyssop
Lavender-English
Lavender- Grosso
Lemon Balm
Marjoram
Marshmallow
Mint
Oregano
Rue
Sage
Skullcap
Southernwood (artemisia)
St. John's Wort
Tarragon
Thyme
Valerian

ZONE 6

Angelica
Anise
Catnip
Chamomile
Chives
Comfrey
Echinacea
Feverfew
Gentian
Hyssop
Lavender-English
Lavender- Grosso
Lemon Balm
Marjoram
Marshmallow
Mint
Oregano
Parsley
Rue
Sage
St. John's Wort
Skullcap
Southernwood (artemisia)
Tarragon
Thyme
Valerian

ZONE 7

Angelica
Anise
Catnip
Chamomile
Chives
Comfrey
Echinacea
Feverfew
Gentian
Hyssop
Lavender-English
Lavender- Grosso
Lemon Balm
Marjoram
Marshmallow
Mint
Oregano
Parsley
Rue
Sage
St. John's Wort
Skullcap
Southernwood (artemisia)
Tarragon
Thyme
Valerian

PERENNIAL HERBS BY ZONE

ZONE 8

- Angelica
- Anise
- Bay Laurel
- Catnip
- Chamomile
- Chives
- Comfrey
- Echinacea
- Eucalyptus
- Feverfew
- Hyssop
- Lavender-English
- Lavender-French
- Lavender-Grosso
- Lavender-Spanish
- Lemon Balm
- Lemon-Verbena
- Marjoram
- Marshmallow
- Mint
- Oregano
- Parsley
- Rosemary
- Rue
- Sage
- St. John's Wort
- Southernwood (artemisia)
- Skullcap
- Tarragon
- Thyme
- Valerian

ZONE 9

- Angelica
- Anise
- Bay Laurel
- Catnip
- Echinacea
- Eucalyptus
- Feverfew
- Ginger
- Hyssop
- Lavender-French
- Lavender- Grosso
- Lavender-Spanish
- Lemon Balm
- Lemon Eucalyptus
- Lemon-Verbena
- Marshmallow
- Mint
- Oregano
- Parsley
- Rosemary
- Rue
- Sage
- Southernwood (artemisia)
- St. John's Wort
- Tarragon
- Thyme
- Valerian

ZONE 10

- Aloe Vera
- Anise
- Bay Laurel
- Echinacea
- Eucalyptus
- Ginger
- Lemon Eucalyptus
- Lemon-Verbena
- Oregano
- Rosemary
- Southernwood

ZONE 11

- Aloe Vera
- Anise
- Eucalyptus
- Ginger
- Lemongrass
- Oregano
- Rosemary
- Stevia
- Southernwood (artemisia)

ZONE 12

- Ginger
- Lemongrass
- Oregano
- Stevia

ZONE 13

- Ginger
- Lemongrass
- Stevia

Herb Growing Differences

- **Annual: only live for one year or growing season.**
- **Perennial: they survive the winter months and come up each spring.**
- **Biennials: produce seeds the year after they are planted and then die.**

The zone you grow in will change if an herb is an annual or perennial.

Some tender perennials can be grown in pots and left out all summer, and brought inside for the winter. Or they can be covered well with straw to protect them from the winter cold. Or they can be dug up each fall and brought inside and then replanted in the spring.

ANNUAL HERBS

Many reseed and grow the next year

Reseeds:	Can grow as annual in zone 3:
Basil	Ginger
Borage	Basil
Calendula	Chervil
Chamomile (German)	Cress
Chervil	Fennel
Chives	Fenugreek
Cilantro	Marjoram
Coriander	Mustard
Dill	Nasturtiums
Fennel	Greek oregano
Horseradish	Marigolds
Marjoram	Rosemary
Oregano	Summer savory
Parsley	Sage
Pot Marigold	French tarragon
Summer Savory	English thyme
Sunflowers	

GROW THESE HERBS FOR PERSONAL USE

Anise Hyssop - Tea	Caraway - Culinary	Dill - Culinary
Lemon Balm - Tea	Lemon Catnip - Tea	Lemongrass - Tea
Lemonella Balm - Tea	Chamomile - Tea	Marjoram - Culinary
Basil - Culinary	Chives - Culinary	Mint - Tea
Bergamot - Tea	Garlic Chives - Culinary	Mustard (brown) - Culinary

Mustard (white) - Culinary	Sage - Culinary
Oregano - Culinary	Summer Savory - Culinary
Parsley - Culinary	Stevia - Tea
Rosemary - Culinary	Thyme - Culinary

Tea Herbs: 1 tsp of dried herb per cup of boiling water.

Cooking: 3 times the amount of fresh herb to equal the dry amount needed. And 1/3 amount less of dry herbs when fresh is called for. Crush dry herbs to release more flavor before adding to the dish.

 Top dress or mix in with grain.

 Dosage balls. Mixing herbs with molasses or peanut butter.

 Mix herbs with olive oil and Thorvin kelp and mix in with grain.

 Make infusion. Steep herbs in just-boiling water, steep for 15 minutes, strain herbs and add the infusion to water buckets.

 Drenching. Mix the dose with water, put in a syringe or drenching gun, and squirt in the back of the mouth over the tongue as far back as possible.

Herbs and holistic treatments are slow working. Their goal is to balance the health of the entire goat, which hopefully will make emergency interventions less necessary. They will help strengthen the immune system when problems do arise.

Be safe in the use of your herbs, used incorrectly or at the wrong times, they can be deadly.

For many recipes start with small doses and increase to about 2 1/2 times the recommended dosage for an adult human. If there are no side effects, up this dosage by 10% (but no higher than 50% of the original dosage). Then increase to up to 3x's per day if needed always watching for adverse effects.

More Herb Growing Tips

- **Usually, the leaves are the most desired part of the herb.**
- **Harvest them just before they start to flower.**
- **For the best flavor, harvest first thing in the morning on a sunny day just after the dew has dried.**
- **To collect seeds, allow them to fully mature and dry. Cut off the entire seed head and stem and place in a plastic bag. Pound the seeds to release them from the plant.**

Herbal Guidelines

Safe Herbs	Blackberry Leaves Cayenne (40,000 heat units) Chamomile Comfrey Dandelion Dill Fennel Flaxseed (Linseed) Garlic Ginger Ivy (Fresh) Kelp Lavender Licorice Lobelia Inflata Marjoram Marshmallow Root	Mullein Nettle Oregano Parsnips Peppermint Red clover Red Raspberry Leaves Rosehips Rosemary Rue Sage Seaweed Senna Southernwood Thyme Wormwood (avoid during pregnancy) Yarrow
Forms of Herbs	Powdered Cut Fresh Tincutres Teas & Infusions	
Factors	Dose based on weight. Herbs are safe, effective and forgiving.	
Frequency	Serious Issue: • Dose every two hours Less Serious: • 3-4 times per day	
Step-Down	Day 1-2: 4 x per day Day 3-4: 3 x per day Day 5: 2 x per day Day 6: 1 x per day Day 7: Reevaluate and stop treatments	

Become educated on each herb you're using before administering.

Herbal Guidelines

DO NOT FEED	Buttercup Greater celandine Foxglove Ragwort Larkspur Deadly nightshade Henbane Wild arum Good King Henry Honeysuckle Morning Glory Bryony (white) Bindweed Bracken Most ferns Winter heliotrope Monkshood Belladonna Greaer Fennel Castorl oil leaves Fruits (in quantity) Yew Laburnum Rhododendron Berries of Laurel Elder Alder

Become educated on each herb you're using before administering.

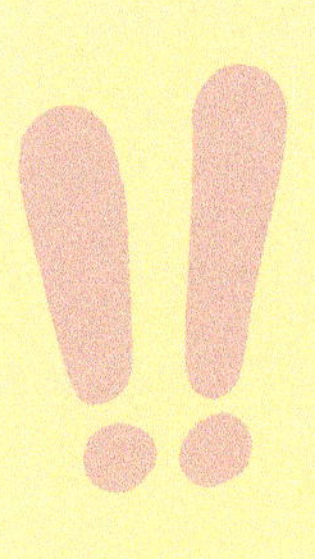

Your goal in treating a sick goat is to keep them alive. If you and your goat are struggling with this natural and herbal process, contact your vet, use their medical advice, which will probably be chemical methods, and then reevaluate your entire feeding and health program and begin again.

Herbal Dosing

Powdered	0-10 lbs 1/8 tsp 11-20 lbs 1/4 tsp 21-40 lbs 1/2 tsp 41-80 lbs 1 tsp 81-150 lbs 1/5-2 tsp
Cut	**General Rule of Thumb:** **Use 2-4 times more than the powdered measurements.**
Fresh	**Double the cut herb dosages.**
Tinctures	**Follow instructions on packaging.**
Homemade Tinctures	0-10 lbs 10 drops / .5 ml 11-20 lbs 20 drops / 1 ml 21-40 lbs 40 drops / 2 ml 41-80 lbs 80 drops / 4 ml 81-150 lbs 150 drops / 7.5 ml

Infusions & Teas	1. Steep in boiling water for 15 minutes.
	2. Cool fully.
	3. Dose directly or allow free choice usage.
	4. Research each herb used to determine dosage.
	5. Steep in one pint boiling water:
	  a. Powdered: 2-3 teaspoons
	  b. Cut: 2 tablespoons
	  c. Fresh: 1/3-1/2 cups
	6. Dosage:
	  a. 0-10 lbs 1.5 tablespoons
	  b. 11-20 lbs 1/4 cup
	  c. 21-40 lbs. 1/2 cup
	  d. 41-80 lbs. 1 cup
	  e. 81-150 lbs. 1 1/4 cups

Become educated on each herb you're using before administering.

HERBAL DEWORMING SUPPORT

Recipes to keep goat's system in optimal shape.

Only use these recipes after reading the following page

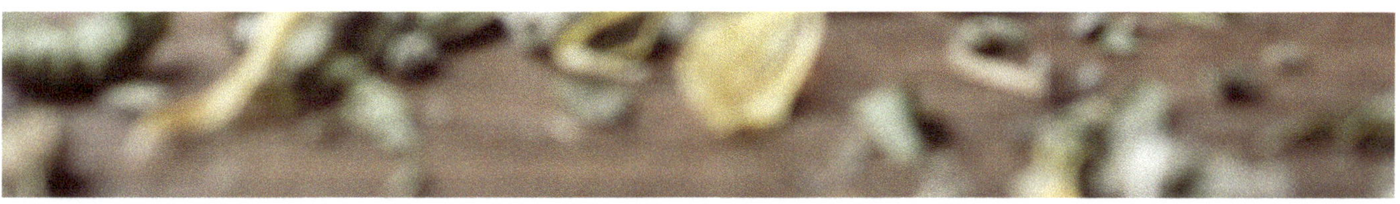

1. These *Herbal Deworming Support* recipes are intended to help goats stay in tip-top shape so they can keep the worms in their bodies in check.

2. But worms are deadly. They are the number one killer of goats.

3. If a goat has an active and unhealthy infestation of worms, they will need chemical dewormers to kill the worms affecting them.

4. Remember to consult with a professional experienced in herbal remedies or a veterinarian who knows about herbal treatments to determine the appropriate dosages and frequency for your goats.

5. Additionally, it's essential to observe your goats closely for any adverse reactions and monitor their fecal egg counts regularly to assess the effectiveness of the herbal deworming support recipes.

While homemade herbal deworming support recipes are a popular addition to chemical dewormers, it's important to note that their effectiveness may vary, and it's recommended to consult with a veterinarian or herbalist for proper guidance. Here are a few recipes for homemade herbal deworming support that you may consider.

Also add to your goat book collection, *My Parasite Control Plan Binder*, so you have all the information needed to effectively control worms in goats.

HERBAL DEWORMER SUPPORT TONIC

* Wormwood is generally considered unsafe during pregnancy.
To be safe, don't give recipes with wormwood to pregnant does.

Ingredients

2 parts dried wormwood (Artemisia absinthium)

1 part dried thyme (Thymus vulgaris)

1 part dried garlic (Allium sativum)

1 part dried fennel seeds (Foeniculum vulgare)

> Wormwood can be left out of main recipe and given individually to the goats who are not pregnant as follows:
>
> Wormwood: 1/4 tsp per 30 pounds.

Directions

1. Mix all the dried herbs in a bowl, ensuring they are well combined.
2. Store the mixture in an airtight container, away from direct sunlight.
3. To administer, mix 1 tablespoon of the herbal mixture per 50 pounds (22 kg) of body weight with your goat's feed once a day for three consecutive days.

DEWORMER SUPPORT HERBAL BALL

Ingredients

- 2 Cups wormwood *
- 2 cups thyme leaf
- 2 cups sage leaf
- 1 cup rosemary leaf powder
- 1 cup psyllium seed powder
- 1 cup mustard seed powder
- 1 cup ginger root powder
- 1 cup garlic (powder or minced) *
- 1 cup cinnamon powder
- 1 cup cayenne pepper powder *
- 1 cup black walnut hull powder *
- 1 cup anise seed powder
- 1/2 cup whole or powdered cloves

- 1/2 cup of the mixture above
- 1/4 cup flour
- 1/4 cup molasses/honey OR
- 1/2-2/3 cup Peanut Butter

Directions

1. Mix all the dried herbs in a bowl, ensuring they are well combined.
2. Store the mixture in an airtight container, away from direct sunlight.
3. Mix 1/2 cup of mixture above with molasses, honey, or peanut butter.
4. Mix and knead dough. Break into 12 pieces, shape into balls, and roll in flour to coat. Each ball is a 2 teaspoon dose. For kids, break the ball into smaller bite-sized pieces.

** Do not give wormwood, or black walnut to pregnant animals!

Wormwood and black walnut can be left out of the main recipe and given individually to the goats who are not pregnant as follows:

Wormwood: 1/4 tsp per 30 pounds.
Black Walnut: 1/8 tsp per 30 pounds.

PUMPKIN SEED DEWORMER SUPPORT

Ingredients

1 cup freshly ground pumpkin seeds

1 tablespoon raw, unfiltered apple cider vinegar

1 tablespoon raw honey

Directions

1. Combine the freshly ground pumpkin seeds, apple cider vinegar, and raw honey in a bowl, mixing well.
2. Administer the mixture directly to your goats orally, using a syringe or mixing it with their feed.
3. The suggested dosage is 1 teaspoon per 10 pounds (4.5 kg) of body weight, given once a day for three consecutive days.

GARLIC BOOST/NATURAL DEWORMER SUPPORT

Ingredients

4 oz finely chopped ginger

4 oz finely chopped garlic

1-2 teaspoons Olive Oil

1/4 cup raw apple cider vinegar

3 tablespoons molasses

2 tablespoons cayenne

1/8 cup hot water

Directions

1. Drizzle olive oil over ginger and garlic and blend until mixed and no chunks.
2. Add remaining ingredients and blend well. This will become a paste.
3. Pour into a jar and store in the fridge for future use.
4. Mix 1 tablespoon of paste with 2 tablespoons of water and fill the drench gun.
5. Use weekly as a preventative to parasites and up to 3x's per day for a sick goat.

HERBAL PELLETS DEWORMER SUPPORT

Ingredients

1 cup of food-grade diatomaceous earth (DE)

1 cup of dried wormwood (Artemisia absinthium)

1 cup of dried thyme (Thymus vulgaris)

1 cup of dried fennel seeds (Foeniculum vulgare)

1 cup of dried garlic (Allium sativum)

> Wormwood can be left out of main recipe and given individually to the goats who are not pregnant as follows:
>
> Wormwood: 1/4 tsp per 30 pounds.

Directions

1. In a bowl, combine the diatomaceous earth, dried herbs, and seeds.
2. Mix well to ensure even distribution.
3. Store the mixture in an airtight container.
4. Offer 1 tablespoon of the herbal dewormer pellets per 50 pounds (22 kg) of body weight to your goats as a natural deworming supplement. You can mix the pellets with their feed or offer them separately.
5. These herbal dewormer pellets provide natural ingredients that are believed to have deworming properties, although their effectiveness may vary. Consult with a veterinarian for guidance on deworming protocols specific to your goat's needs.

GARLIC & HERB DEWORMING SUPPORT TINCTURE

Ingredients

1 part dried garlic (Allium sativum)

1 part dried wormwood (Artemisia absinthium)

1 part dried thyme (Thymus vulgaris)

Vodka or apple cider vinegar (enough to cover the herbs)

Wormwood can be left out of main recipe and given individually to the goats who are not pregnant as follows:

Wormwood: 1/4 tsp per 30 pounds.

Directions

1. Combine the dried herbs in a jar and pour enough vodka or apple cider vinegar over them to cover.
2. Seal the jar tightly and store it in a cool, dark place for at least two weeks, shaking it occasionally.
3. After two weeks, strain the liquid, discard the solids, and transfer the tincture to a dark glass bottle.
4. Administer 1 teaspoon per 25 pounds (11 kg) of body weight, mixed with water or added to feed, once a day for three consecutive days.

KID HEALTH BOOSTER
SCOUR PREVENTION

Ingredients

Cinnamon powder

Ginger powder

Slippery elm OR marshmallow root

Garlic powder

Clove powder

Cayenne powder (1/2 part)

Directions

1. Mix equal parts of the ingredients except cayenne powder which will be a 1/2 part.
2. 1/4 tsp can be added to bottles for bottle babies to prevent cocci, scours, parasites, and enterotoxemia.

CLOVER HERBAL DEWORMER SUPPORT

Ingredients

- Fennel Seed
- Oregano
- Dehydrated garlic
- Sage
- Thyme
- Pumpkin seed
- Red clover
- Hyssop

Directions

1. Mix in equal parts by volume and not weight.
2. Mix 1 tablespoon with one tablespoon Diatomaceous earth and mix into a daily ration of grain.
3. Repeat weekly.

IMMUNE BOOSTING

Boost a Goat's Health to a New Level

ELECTROLYTE SOLUTION

You'll be surprised at how easy it is to make your own electrolytes at home!

Ingredients

1 quart of warm water

2 tablespoons of raw honey

1 teaspoon of sea salt

1 teaspoon of baking soda

Directions

- Mix all the ingredients until they are dissolved.

- Offer this electrolyte solution to goats who are experiencing dehydration, heat stress, or recovering from illness to help replenish their electrolyte balance.

HOMEMADE PROBIOTIC PASTE

Boost that beneficial gut bacteria...in yourself and your goat!

Ingredients

1 cup of plain, unsweetened yogurt (preferably raw or homemade)

1 teaspoon of raw honey

1 teaspoon of apple cider vinegar

Directions

- Mix all the ingredients thoroughly to create a smooth paste.

- Offer this probiotic paste to your goats to support their digestive health and boost beneficial gut bacteria. Administer a small amount orally or mix it with their feed as a supplement.

HERBAL IMMUNE BOOSTER

Helps a goat during stress or illness.

Ingredients

1 part echinacea (Echinacea purpurea) root

1 part elderberry (Sambucus nigra) berries

1 part rosehips (Rosa canina)

1 part dried nettle (Urtica dioica) leaf

Directions

- Mix the herbs together and store them in an airtight container.

- Add 1 teaspoon per 50 pounds (22 kg) of body weight to your goat's feed daily for immune system support during times of stress or illness.

Unripe elderberries are potentially very dangerous, and should be avoided at all costs.

HERBAL IMMUNE BOOSTER

Helps a goat during stress or illness.

Ingredients

Garlic

Echinacea

Goldenseal

Rosehips

Directions

- Mix the herbs in equal parts and store in an airtight container.
- Add 1 teaspoon per 50 pounds (22 kg) of body weight to your goat's feed daily for immune system support during times of stress or illness.

Unripe elderberries are potentially very dangerous, and should be avoided at all costs.

BOOST THAT IMMUNITY

Helps a goat during stress
or illness.

Ingredients

Fenugreek

Garlic

Echinacea

Astragalus

Directions

- Mix equal parts of herbs together and store in an
  airtight container.
- Use 1-2 tablespoons, 2 times per day.

GARLIC & APPLE CIDER VINEGAR DRENCH

Ingredients

2 cloves of fresh garlic (Allium sativum), minced

1 tablespoon of raw, unfiltered apple cider vinegar

1 cup of water

Helps a goat during stress or illness.

Directions

- Combine the minced garlic, apple cider vinegar, and water in a bowl.
- Allow the mixture to steep for several hours or overnight.
- Strain the liquid and administer orally as a drench to help support overall health and promote parasite resistance.
- Adjust the dosage according to your goat's weight, following veterinary advice.
- Remember, while these natural remedies can be beneficial, it's important to consult with a veterinarian or experienced herbalist to ensure they are appropriate for your specific goat's needs. They can provide further guidance on dosages, frequency, and potential interactions with other treatments or health conditions.

GARLIC TEA

Prevent tetanus and infection.

Ingredients

Garlic

Echinacea

Goldenseal

Directions

- Cover crushed garlic with hot water and let steep over several hours or overnight.
- Add equal parts echinacea and goldenseal to the water mixture and bring to a boil.
- Strain the liquid.
- Administer orally as a drench or add to a kid's bottle.

KNOCK DOWN & OUT

Knock down sickness & knock out worms

Ingredients

4 oz finely chopped ginger

4 oz finely chopped garlic

1-2 teaspoons Olive Oil

1/4 Cup raw apple cider vinegar

3 Tablespoons molasses

2 Tablespoons cayenne

1/8 cup hot water

Directions

- Drizzle olive oil over ginger and garlic and blend until mixed and no chunks.
- Add remaining ingredients and blend well. This will become a paste.
- Pour into a jar and store in the fridge for future use.
- Mix 1 tablespoon of paste with 2 tablespoons of water and fill drench gun.
- Use weekly as a preventative to parasites and up to 3x's per day for a sick goat.

ANTIBACTERIAL

Fight the Infections Naturally

GARLIC INFUSION

Garlic is powerful and can aid in mastitis prevention, respiratory issues, parasite control, and has antibacterial properties.

Ingredients

Fresh garlic cloves (crushed or minced)

Olive oil

Directions

- Combine fresh minced garlic cloves with enough olive oil to cover them.
- Let the mixture sit for several days to allow the garlic to infuse into the oil.
- Strain the mixture to remove the garlic solids.
- Apply the garlic-infused oil topically to wounds or skin infections as a natural antibacterial ointment.
- Garlic has antimicrobial properties and can help inhibit the growth of bacteria. However, it's essential to consult with a veterinarian to determine the appropriate use and dosage for your specific goat.

HONEY & TURMERIC POULTICE

This combination is easy to make but very effective.

Ingredients

Raw honey

Turmeric powder

Directions

- Mix raw honey and turmeric powder to create a thick paste.
- Apply the paste to wounds, abscesses, or skin infections as a poultice.
- Cover the affected area with a clean, sterile dressing.
- Replace the poultice and dressing regularly.
- Both honey and turmeric possess antimicrobial and anti-inflammatory properties. However, it's crucial to consult with a veterinarian to ensure appropriate wound management and determine if additional veterinary care or antibiotics are necessary.
- Remember, natural remedies should be used as supportive measures and should never replace professional veterinary care. It's important to work closely with a veterinarian who can diagnose the specific condition and prescribe appropriate treatments, including antibiotics, when necessary.

GARLIC & HONEY PASTE

Soothing and Antimicrobial.

Ingredients

3 cloves of fresh garlic

1 tablespoon of raw honey

Directions

- Crush the garlic cloves to create a paste.
- Mix the garlic paste with the raw honey until well combined.
- Administer a small amount of the garlic and honey paste orally to your goat once or twice daily.
- Garlic is believed to possess antimicrobial properties, while honey may provide soothing effects.

MASTITIS TREATMENT

As shared in "The Complete Herbal Handbook for Farm and Stable"

Ingredients

Water

Molasses

Epsom Salts

Linseed oil

Ground ginger

Grated gentian root

Oatmeal gruel

Eucaluptus oil

Dock leaves

Directions

- 2 days the goat is on water only, or a solution of water and molasses.
- On both of those nights, give the goat a purge to eat: 2 ounces of Epsom Salts, 1 ounce of linseed oil, half a teaspoon of ground ginger, 1 teaspoonful of grated gentian root, and 2 ounces of warm water. Mix this in an oatmeal gruel to make 1.5 pints.
- Also, use hot applications of a few drops of eucalyptus oil added to a hot brew of dock leaves. Use deep and gentle pressure applied by the fingers to help expel the matter that's causing hardness in the udder and teats.

MASTITIS REMEDY

These herbs will help fight off mastitis!

Ingredients

Lobelia

Mullein

Garlic

Directions

- Equal parts of each.
- Top dress grain if they will eat the herbs.
- Or make a brew of the ingredients with 1.5 pints of water, allow to cool, and drench several times a day.

TEAT WASH

Keep it clean! And it's easy to do!

Ingredients

20 drops lavender oil

10 drops tea Trea oil

2 tablespoons liquid Castile soap

Directions

- Fill a Quart-sized spray bottle with warm water. Add ingredients and shake well.
- Spray teats after milking to prevent bacteria.
- Add peppermint to help encourage milk letdown and engorged udders.

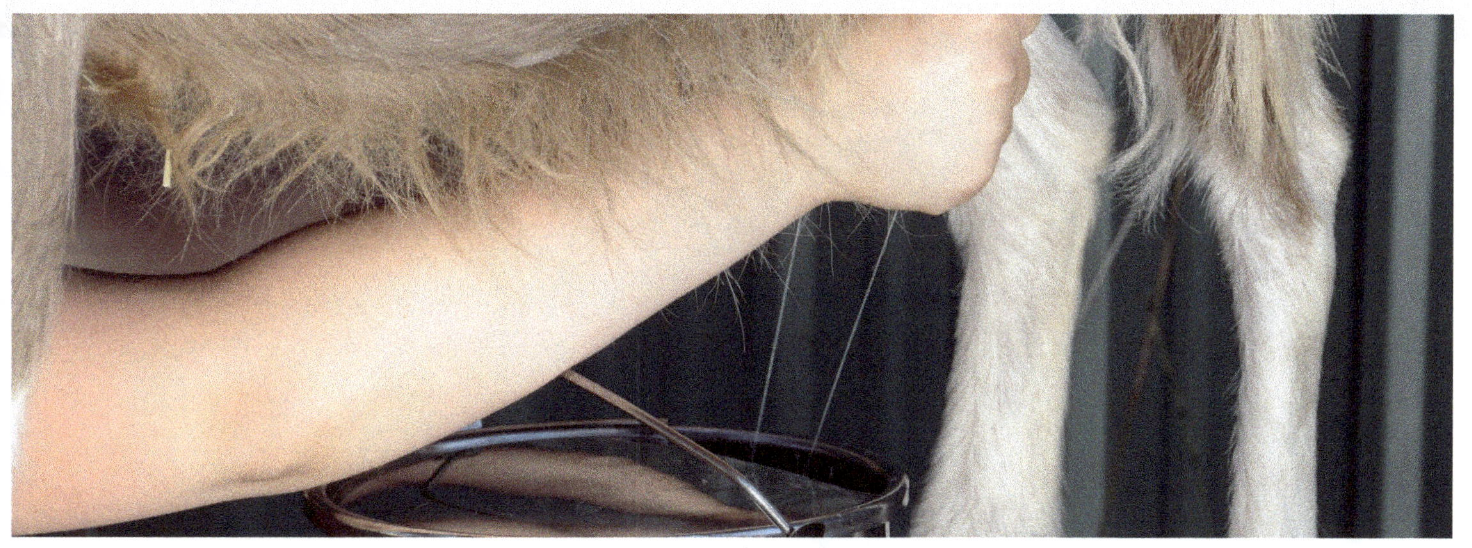

WOUND TREATMENT

Healing wound spray.

Ingredients

Apple cider vinegar

Aloe vera juice

Tea tree oil

Strong tea from calendula and echinacea

Directions

- Mix equal parts of each ingredient.
- Add to spray bottle.
- Spray affected area several times a day.

ELDERBERRY SKIN WASH

And excellent wash for skin ailments.

Ingredients

3 handfuls of elderberry leaves

1 handful of wild geranium plant

1 root of garlic

Directions

- Grate the garlic
- Cut the elder and geranium finely
- Add to a quart of water and bring to a boil.
- Simmer for 20 minutes, then brew for 4 hours.
- Keep covered.
- Bathe affected areas twice daily.
- Can also give 1 cup internally for fevers.

POULTICES & WOUND CARE

Remember to consult with a professional experienced in herbal remedies or a veterinarian who knows about herbal treatments to determine the appropriate dosages and frequency for your goats. Additionally, it's essential to observe your goats closely for any adverse reactions or worsening conditions.

Fresh Herb Poultice Instructions

- Estimate how many herbs you will need. The size of the affected area will help you determine how much to make.
- Chop the herbs into small pieces.
- Transfer to a mortar and pestle and begin to crush the herbs until they are pulp.
- Continue to mash until they are very smooth. The juices of the herbs will begin to flow and when this happens, the plant is beginning to release their natural juices.
- You may also use a blender instead of chopping and using a mortar and pestle.
- Spread the mixture over the affected area.
- Wrap it with gauze or muslin to hold it in place.

Dried Herb Poultice Instructions

- Estimate how many herbs you will need. The size of the affected area will help you determine how much to make.
- Combine with enough hot water to moisten them and create a thick paste.
- If using roots, it's best if they are powdered.
- Spread the paste evenly over the problem area.
- Wrap with gauze or muslin.

COMFREY POULTICE

Comfrey is a must in your herbal cabinet.

Ingredients

Dried comfrey leaves

Hot water

Directions

- Crush or grind the dried comfrey leaves into a coarse powder.
- Place the powdered comfrey leaves in a bowl and add hot water to form a thick paste.
- Allow the mixture to cool slightly.
- Apply the comfrey poultice directly to the affected area, such as wounds, sprains, or swellings.
- Cover the poultice with a clean cloth or gauze and secure it in place.
- Leave the poultice on for 1-2 hours before gently removing it.
- Repeat the application as needed, usually once or twice a day, until improvement is observed.
- Comfrey has soothing and healing properties and is often used to support tissue repair. However, it's important to note that comfrey should not be used on open wounds or used for an extended period without veterinary guidance, as it contains compounds that may be harmful if ingested.

CALENDULA POULTICE

Calendula is so easy to grow!

Ingredients

Dried calendula flowers

Hot water

Directions

- Crush or grind the dried calendula flowers into a coarse powder.
- Place the powdered calendula flowers in a bowl and add hot water to form a paste.
- Allow the mixture to cool slightly.
- Apply the calendula poultice directly to skin irritations, wounds, or inflammations.
- Cover the poultice with a clean cloth or gauze and secure it in place.
- Leave the poultice on for 1-2 hours before gently removing it.
- Repeat the application as needed, usually once or twice a day, until improvement is observed.
- Calendula is known for its anti-inflammatory and wound-healing properties, making it a commonly used herb for skin conditions. It can help soothe irritations and support the healing process.

HERBAL POULTICE

Always have your healing herbs ready for any accident that may occur!

Ingredients

1/4 cup of dried calendula flowers

1/4 cup of dried comfrey leaves

1/4 cup of dried plantain leaves

Water (enough to make a paste)

Directions

- Grind the dried herbs into a fine powder using a mortar and pestle or a clean coffee grinder.
- Transfer the powdered herbs to a bowl and slowly add water while stirring to create a thick paste.
- Apply the herbal poultice directly to wounds or skin irritations on your goat, covering the affected area.
- Leave the poultice in place for several hours or overnight, then gently remove and clean the area.
- Repeat the application as needed to support healing and provide natural wound care.
- These homemade herbal recipes for goats can be a beneficial addition to their care routine. However, it's important to note that individual goat needs may vary, and it's always advisable to consult with a veterinarian or herbalist who is familiar with goats to ensure the safety and appropriateness of the herbs for your specific goat's needs.

BAG BALM

A timeless recipe.

Ingredients

1/4 cup beeswax

1 cup shea butter

1/2 cup coconut oil

1/4 cup olive oil

5-10 drops tea tree essential oil

5-10 drops lavender essential oil

*Peppermint essential oil can be added. Helps with letdown.

Directions

- In a double boiler, melt the beeswax, shea butter, coconut oil, and olive oil together.
- Add essential oils to the mixture and stir well.
- Pour into a shatterproof container that can withstand heat (like a canning jar) and allow time to solidify.
- Use on goat's udder to moisturize and protect.

HEALING POULTICE

Herbs to heal.

Ingredients

1 cup of dried or fresh herbs of your choice (such as chamomile, calendula, comfrey, or plantain)

1/2 cup of hot water

2 tablespoons of bentonite clay (optional)

Clean cloth or gauze

Directions

- Place the herbs in a bowl and pour hot water over them. Let it steep for about 10 minutes to allow the herbs to release their beneficial properties.
- If using bentonite clay, add it to the herbal infusion and mix well until you have a smooth paste.
- Let the mixture cool down to a comfortable temperature.
- Once the poultice is at a suitable temperature, apply it directly to the affected area. For humans, you can apply it to wounds, bruises, insect bites, rashes, or swollen joints. For animals, apply it to wounds, abscesses, inflammation, or areas with skin irritations.
- Spread the poultice evenly over the affected area to form a thick layer.
- Cover the poultice with a clean cloth or gauze to keep it in place and protect it from drying out.
- Leave the poultice on for 1 to 2 hours, or as directed by a healthcare professional or veterinarian.
- After the recommended time, remove the poultice and gently clean the area with warm water.
- Dispose of the used poultice and wash the cloth or gauze for future use.
- Note: It's important to consult with a healthcare professional or veterinarian before applying a poultice, especially if you're unsure about the suitability of certain herbs or if the condition worsens.

CLEANSING POULTICE

Basic healing poultice with readily available ingredients.

Ingredients

Burdock root

Dandelion leaves

Directions

- Estimate how much you will need to cover the wound and affected area.
- Create a poultice following the steps at the beginning of this chapter.
- Spread the mixture evenly on the area of concern. Wrap with gaze to hold in place.
- Change several times throughout the day.

BLACK WALNUT SALVE

A healing salve

Ingredients

2 unripe black walnuts

2 tablespoons olive oil

2 tablespoons cocoa butter or shea butter

2 tablespoons softened beeswax

Directions

- In a mortar and pestle, grind and pound the outer, green husks of two unripe walnuts until it is mushy.
- Add to a non-aluminum pan.
- Add olive oil and cocoa or shea butter.
- Turn on low heat and heat for 1 hour, stirring frequently. Do not boil or overheat.
- Strain the mixture and then squeeze out the excess oils.
- Add oils back into the pan then add the beeswax and mix until completely melted.
- Scoop out a small amount into a spoon and allow it to cool. If it is too thin, add more beeswax and if too thick, add more olive oil.
- Pour into wide-mouth jars and store in a cool, dark place.
- Makes about 3 ounces.
- Apply liberally to the affected area several times a day.

ELDER BLOSSOM SALVE

A healing salve

Ingredients

Olive oil

Beeswax

Nut fat (animals don't like the fat of dead animals rubbed on them)

Directions

- Add equal parts of each and slowly heat until fully dissolved.
- Make about 1 pint worth of oil.
- Put as much finely chopped elderberry leaves and blossoms in as it will absorb.
- Stir well for ten minutes.
- Add to jars, put on lids, and allow to set.
- Apply to wounds, sores, bruises, and ulcers.

GINGER, GARLIC PASTE

Boost that immune system and natural dewormer.

Ingredients

3 tablespoon cayenne

3 tablespoons black strap molasses

1/4 cup apple cider vinegar

Olive oil

4 ounces finely chopped garlic

4 ouces finely chopped ginger

Directions

- Blend garlic and ginger with a little olive oil until it is smooth and creamy.
- Add the remaining ingredients and blend well.
- Add to 1/8 cup of hot water. Shake to incorporate well and add to a jar with a non-corrosive lid.
- Keep it in the fridge.
- Add 2 tablespoons of water to 2 tablespoons of paste. This will allow it to be pulled up into a drench gun or syringe.
- You can use this for maintenance once a week.
- When a goat is sick, use it 3 times a day.

SLIPPERY ELM POULTICE

Great for wounds and areas of swelling.

Ingredients

Slippery elm powder

Egg whites

Directions

- Make a paste with an egg white and slippery elm powder.
- Make enough for the affected area.
- Paint over affected areas

- Place the powder in a flannel patch, fold carefully over the powder, and boil for 5 minutes. then lay the flannel on the affected area.

ENERGY BOOSTING

Tonic, support, treats.

OVERALL WELL−BEING

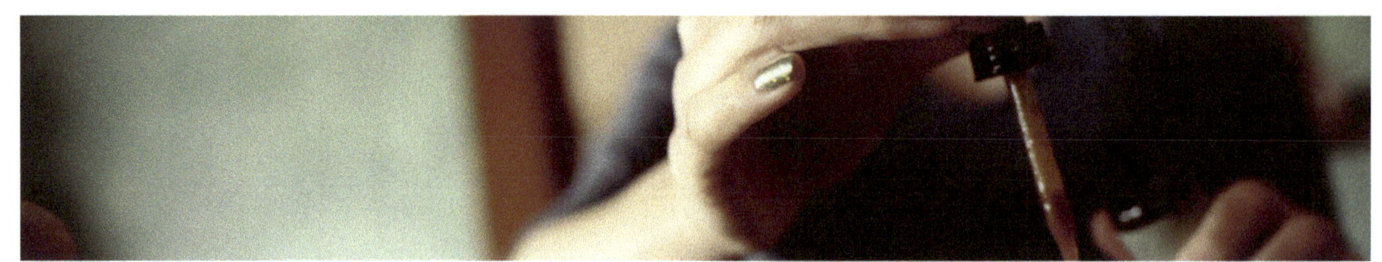

ENERGY BOOSTING TONIC

Improve and boost energy.

You'll be surprised at how conveniently you can make this tonic at home.

Ingredients

1 cup of unsweetened apple cider vinegar

1 cup of molasses

1 tablespoon of raw honey

1 teaspoon of powdered kelp

1 teaspoon of powdered spirulina

1 teaspoon of powdered alfalfa

Directions

- In a bowl, combine the apple cider vinegar, molasses, raw honey, powdered kelp, spirulina, and alfalfa.
- Mix the ingredients thoroughly until well blended.
- Store the mixture in a dark, airtight container.
- Add 1 tablespoon of the energy-boosting tonic to each goat's daily feed ration, or mix it with water and administer it orally.
- Continue the supplementation for a period of time as recommended by your veterinarian or until you see an improvement in the goat's energy levels.

This homemade tonic contains ingredients that provide essential nutrients, minerals, and antioxidants to support energy production and overall vitality in goats. Apple cider vinegar can help improve digestion and nutrient absorption, molasses provides a natural source of sugars for quick energy, raw honey contains enzymes and antioxidants, and kelp, spirulina, and alfalfa are nutrient-rich supplements known for their energy-boosting properties.

However, it's important to note that individual goat needs may vary, and it's always advisable to consult with a veterinarian or nutritionist who can provide specific recommendations based on your goat's health status, age, and dietary requirements.

Additionally, ensure that the goats have access to clean water, high-quality forage, and a balanced diet to support their overall energy levels and well-being.

HERBAL GOAT TONIC

Keep the well-being in your goat.

Nutrients and overall health support.

Ingredients

2 parts dried nettle (Urtica dioica) leaf

1 part dried raspberry (Rubus idaeus) leaf

1 part dried chamomile (Matricaria chamomilla) flowers

1 part dried dandelion (Taraxacum officinale) leaf

Directions

- Mix the dried herbs together in a bowl, ensuring they are well combined.
- Store the mixture in an airtight container, away from direct sunlight.
- To use, steep 1 tablespoon of the herbal mixture in 1 cup of hot water for 10-15 minutes.
- Allow the infusion to cool, then offer it to your goat as a natural tonic. You can mix it with their water or administer it directly.

This herbal tonic provides a variety of beneficial nutrients and can support overall health and well-being in goats.

HOMEMADE GOAT TREAT

We all need a healthy treat, even the goats!

Yes, you have permission to spoil your goats just a little bit!

Ingredients

2 cups of rolled oats

1 cup of mashed bananas

1 tablespoon of raw honey

1 tablespoon of peanut butter

   (make sure it doesn't contain xylitol,

   which is toxic to goats)

Directions

- Preheat the oven to 350°F (175°C).
- In a bowl, combine the rolled oats, mashed bananas, raw honey, and peanut butter, mixing well.
- Roll the mixture into small balls and place them on a baking sheet lined with parchment paper.
- Bake for 10-12 minutes or until the treats are lightly golden.
- Allow the treats to cool before offering them to your goats as a healthy and natural snack.

These homemade treats are a nutritious and tasty option for rewarding your goats and can be used for training or simply as a special treat.

GARLIC & APPLE CIDER VINEGAR WATER

Hydration with some immune boosting goodness!

Hydration is a key factor in a goat's health. Keep them hydrated and healthy!

Ingredients

1 clove of fresh garlic (Allium sativum), minced

1 tablespoon of raw, unfiltered apple cider vinegar

1 gallon (3.8 liters) of clean drinking water

Directions

- In a clean container, add the minced garlic, apple cider vinegar, and water.
- Mix well to ensure the ingredients are evenly distributed.
- Allow the mixture to sit for a few hours to infuse.
- Offer this garlic and apple cider vinegar water to your goats as a natural immune booster and overall health supplement.

Garlic and apple cider vinegar are known for their potential immune-boosting and health-supportive properties.

HERBAL HOOF SOAK

Without a strong, healthy hoof, the goat has nothing.

Keep your goat's hooves healthy before the injury happens!

Directions

Ingredients

1 clove of fresh garlic (Allium sativum), minced

1 tablespoon of raw, unfiltered apple cider vinegar

1 gallon (3.8 liters) of clean water

- In a large bucket or container, add the dried herbs to the warm water
- Allow the mixture to steep for 30 minutes.
- Soak the goat's hooves in the herbal infusion for 10-15 minutes.
- Gently dry the hooves afterward. This herbal soak can help promote healthy hooves and support hoof health.

NOURISHING HERBAL MASH

Variety in a goat's diet is a key to their health.

Put aside the processed treats and give your goats a treat that makes them feel good!

Ingredients

2 cups of rolled oats

1 cup of barley

1 cup of flaxseed meal

1 cup of dried alfalfa leaves

1 tablespoon of dried nettle leaf

Directions

- Cook the rolled oats and barley according to their package instructions.
- In a bowl, mix the cooked oats and barley with the flaxseed meal, dried alfalfa leaf, and dried nettle leaf.
- Allow the mixture to cool and offer it as a nourishing herbal mash to your goats as a treat or supplement.

CALMING HERBAL BLEND

Calm when they need it most.

Goats are easily stressed. Give them some calm in the moment they need it.

Ingredients

1 tablespoon of dried chamomile flowers

1 tablespoon of dried lemon balm leaves

1 tablespoon of dried skullcap leaves

Directions

- Mix the dried herbs together in a bowl.
- Steep 1 tablespoon of the herbal mixture in 1 cup of hot water for 10-15 minutes.
- Allow the infusion to cool and offer it to your goat as a calming herbal blend. You can mix it with their water or administer it orally.

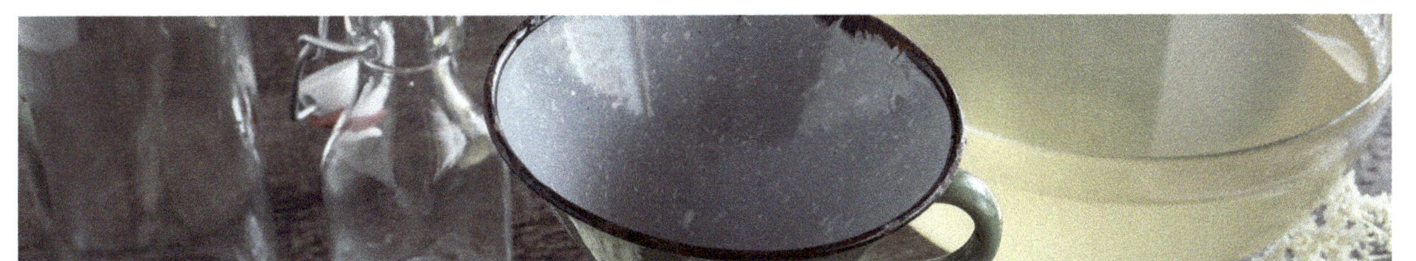

RESPIRATORY SUPPORT TEA

Keep those lungs healthy!

Provide your goat with the support needed to maintain healthy lungs in a world where there are a lot of unnecessary and unhealthy inputs.

Ingredients

Eucalyptus

Thyme

Rosemary

Peppermint

Directions

- Mix 1-3 drops in a pot of boiling water.
- Put a towel over the goat's head and the bowl under their nose and let the steam rise up to breathe for 3-5 minutes.
- Allow oxygen to enter under the tent, to allow for easier breathing as they breathe in the steam.

HERBAL STRESS RELIEF TINCTURE

Stress can be mitigated for the easily stressed goat!

Goats will handle stress much better if we help them through the times that cause them angst.

Ingredients

1/4 cup of dried chamomile flowers

1/4 cup of dried lemon balm leaves

1/4 cup of dried passion flower leaves

1 cup of vodka or brandy

Directions

- In a glass jar, combine the dried herbs and vodka or brandy.
- Ensure the herbs are fully submerged in the liquid.
- Seal the jar tightly and place it in a cool, dark place for at least 4-6 weeks, shaking the jar occasionally.
- After the steeping period, strain the liquid, discarding the herbal residue.
- Administer 1-2 teaspoons of the herbal stress relief tincture

COOLING HERBAL SPRAY

Cool and refresh your goat.

The cooling affect will bring instant relief.

Ingredients

1 cup of aloe vera gel

1 cup of distilled water

10 drops of peppermint essential oil

10 drops of lavender essential oil

5 drops of eucalyptus essential oil

Directions

- In a spray bottle, combine the aloe vera gel and distilled water.
- Add the peppermint, lavender, and eucalyptus essential oils to the mixture.
- Shake well to ensure all ingredients are thoroughly blended.
- Spray the cooling herbal mixture onto your goat's coat during hot weather or after physical activity to provide a refreshing and cooling sensation.

SICK GOAT REMEDIES

Act quickly! Immediately!

DOWN GOAT RECIPE

Energy + Strength

Ingredients

---

1 baked sweet potato
1 can of ripe, stout beer
1/4 cup molasses
1 cup yogurt
1 cup water

Directions

Blend ingredients until it has a soup-like consistency. If the goat is unwilling to eat it, it can be force-fed.

Feed until the goat is well and eating normally.

From Ken Gossard of Dairygoatforum

RESPIRATOR SUPPORT HERBAL STEAM

Support

Ingredients

2 tablespoons of dried eucalyptus leaves

2 tablespoons of dried thyme leaves

1 tablespoon of dried peppermint leaves

1 quart (946 ml) of boiling water

Directions

In a large heatproof bowl, add the dried leaves.

Pour the boiling water over the herbs.

Place a towel over your goat's head and the bowl, creating a tent to trap the steam.

Allow your goat to inhale the herbal steam for a few minutes, providing respiratory support.

CAYENNE TINCTURE

Soothe+ Relieve + Fight

Ingredients

3 Cups apple cider vinegar or Vodka
1 Cup cayenne.

Directions

Mix ingredients.

Let sit and cure for 4 weeks.

Strain and store in a cool place.

Dose by weight:
100-200 Pounds: 1 tsp 2-4 times
daily

Cayenne is used primarily to stop bleeding, soothe stings and bites, and relieve arthritis pain.

Internally, it was used to help both lower and raise blood pressure, fight infections, help heal ulcers, and create an environment where worms won't thrive.

SICK GOAT RECIPE

Energy + Life

Ingredients

1/4 cup molasses
1/4 cup milk kefir
1 clove garlic
2-4 tablespoons apple cider vinegar

Directions

Blend ingredients well in a jar.

Use a drenchiing gun and suck up 30 ccs of the liquid. Place at the back of tongue and feed to your sick goat.

Repeat 3 times a day until energy and life has returned to the goat.

UPSET RUMEN RECIPE

Prevent + Boost

Ingredients

1 cup water
2 tablespoons molasses
1/2 cup apple cider vinegar
2 tablespoons fresh ginger
2 tablespoons cinnamon
2 tablespoons cayenne pepper
Probios

Directions

Blend ingredients well in a jar.

Offer to sick goat, if they won't drink it, use a syringe or bolus gun and give at the back of the tongue.

This recipe will keep a goat hydrated and will boost their gut health.

HOMEMADE NUTRI-DRENCH

Revive - Restore

Ingredients

1 Cup corn oil
1 Cup Molasses
1 Cup Karo Syrup

Directions

Mix ingredients into a jar

Drench several doses every two hours throughout the day until the goat's energy has returned to normal.

SCOURS TREATMENT

Stop + Clear

Ingredients

1 tsp Powdered slippery elm
1/4 cup water

Directions

Mix powdered slippery elm mixed into water. Shake jar vigorously until well blended.

Drench goat three times a day with above mixture.

Continue to give to the goat 2-3 days after the scours have cleared up.

HEALTHY HAIR

Start with top quality health and then add some shine

A shiny hair coat in goats can be achieved by providing a balanced diet, good grooming practices, and incorporating certain natural ingredients known for promoting healthy skin and coats. Here are a few natural recipes that may help improve the shine of your goat's hair coat.

FLAXSEED OIL

Get some shine in your goat's hair!

Ingredients

1 Tablespoon Flaxseed Oil Supplement

Directions

- Add 1 tablespoon of flaxseed oil to your goat's daily feed ration.
- Mix well to ensure it is evenly distributed.
- Flaxseed oil is rich in omega-3 fatty acids, which can help improve skin and coat health, leading to a shinier hair coat.
- Note: Ensure the flaxseed oil is fresh and stored properly to prevent rancidity.

HERBAL RINSE

A final rinse that smells delightful!

Ingredients

2 cups of water

1 tablespoon of dried rosemary

1 tablespoon of dried lavender

Directions

- Boil the water and add the dried rosemary and lavender.
- Allow the herbs to steep in the hot water for about 30 minutes.
- Strain the mixture and let it cool to room temperature.
- Use the herbal infusion as a final rinse after bathing your goat, pouring it over their coat, or using a spray bottle.
- Gently massage the rinse into the coat and let it air dry.
- Rosemary and lavender are known for their soothing properties and their potential to promote a healthy hair coat.

ACV SPRAY

Restore healthy and shiny hair coat!

Ingredients

1 cup of raw, unfiltered apple cider vinegar

1 cup of water

5 drops of lavender essential oil (optional)

Directions

- Mix the apple cider vinegar and water in a spray bottle.
- Optional: Add a few drops of lavender essential oil for a pleasant scent.
- Shake the mixture well to combine the ingredients.
- Spray the diluted apple cider vinegar solution onto your goat's coat, avoiding the eyes and sensitive areas.
- Gently brush or massage the mixture into the hair coat to promote shine and reduce odor.
- Apple cider vinegar helps restore the pH balance of the skin, which can contribute to a healthy and shiny hair coat.

DIGESTION

Cornerstone of Health

The most important aspect of your goat's health is their digestive system. It is imperative that you feed them properly, give them minerals, and watch for any digestive changes that may occur.

It is imperative you act quickly when they get sick
or are showing signs of discomfort.

DIGESTIVE SUPPORT HERBAL SYRUP

Ingredients

1 cup of dried peppermint leaves

1 cup of dried fennel seeds

1 cup of dried chamomile flowers

4 cups of water

1 cup of raw honey

Directions

- In a saucepan, add the dried herbs and water.
- Simmer the mixture on low heat for 20-30 minutes.
- Strain the liquid and discard the herbs.
- Return the herbal infusion to the saucepan and add the raw honey.
- Stir well until the honey is fully dissolved.
- Allow the herbal syrup to cool before transferring it to a glass jar or bottle.
- Offer 1-2 tablespoons of digestive support herbal syrup to your goat as needed to promote healthy digestion and soothe the digestive system.

HERBAL DIGESTION TEA

Ingredients

1 tablespoon of blackberry leaves

1 tablespoon of raspberry leaves

1 tablespoon of oak bark

1 liter of water

Directions

- In a saucepan, bring the water to a boil.
- Add the blackberry leaves, raspberry leaves, and oak bark to the boiling water.
- Reduce the heat and let the mixture simmer for about 10 minutes.
- Remove the saucepan from heat and allow the herbal tea to cool.
- Strain the tea to remove the herb particles.
- Offer the herbal tannin tea to your goat to drink.
- Continue offering the tea for 24-48 hours or as directed by a veterinarian.

These recipes are intended for temporary relief of mild diarrhea. If the diarrhea persists, worsens, or is accompanied by other concerning symptoms, it's crucial to seek veterinary assistance promptly for proper diagnosis and treatment.

FLY CONTROL

Store-bought chemicals no more!

HERBAL FLY SPRAY

Keep those flies away!

An easy and natural recipe to keep flies away!

Ingredients

1 cup of apple cider vinegar

1 cup of water

10 drops of lavender essential oil

10 drops of citronella essential oil

5 drops of eucalyptus essential oil

Directions

- In a spray bottle, combine the apple cider vinegar and water.
- Add the lavender, citronella, and eucalyptus essential oils to the mixture.
- Shake well to ensure the ingredients are thoroughly mixed.
- Use the herbal fly spray to repel flies and insects from your goat's coat. Apply as needed, avoiding the eyes and sensitive areas.

HERBAL FLY REPELLENT SALVE

Repel flies in exposed areas

Flies are relentless, so keep them off of the sensitive areas.

Ingredients

1/2 cup of coconut oil

2 tablespoons of neem oil

10 drops of eucalyptus essential oil

10 drops of lavender essential oil

10 drops of citronella essential oil

10 drops of tea tree essential oil

Directions

- In a small saucepan, melt the coconut oil over low heat.
- Remove from heat and add the neem oil, eucalyptus essential oil, lavender essential oil, citronella essential oil, and tea tree essential oil.
- Stir well to ensure all ingredients are thoroughly combined.
- Allow the mixture to cool and solidify.
- Apply a small amount of the fly-repellent salve to exposed areas of your goat's body to repel flies and insects.

REPELLENT HERBAL COLLAR

It goes where the goat goes!

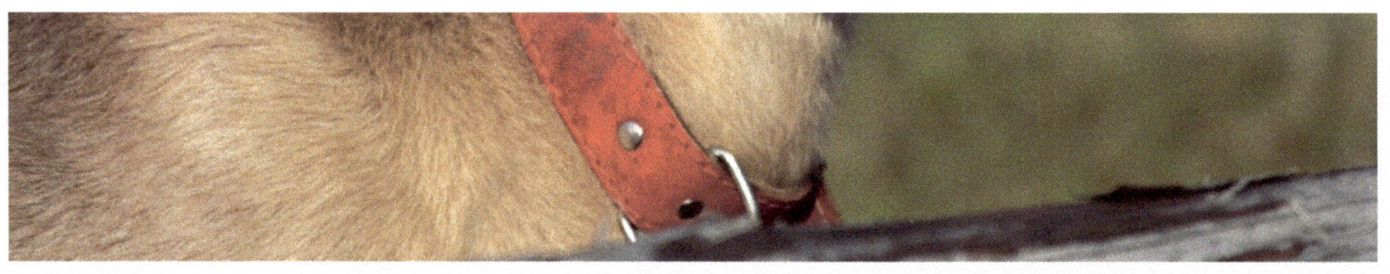

This is a great solution through the summer fly season.

Ingredients

Strip of fabric

10 drops of cedarwood essential oil

10 drops of lemongrass essential oil

10 drops of rosemary essential oil

Directions

- Lay the fabric strip flat.
- Combine the cedar wood, lemongrass, and rosemary essential oils in a small bowl.
- Dip your fingers or a cotton ball into the essential oil mixture and rub it onto the fabric.
- Allow the fabric to dry completely before tying it around your goat's neck as a natural repellent collar. Refresh the essential oil every few weeks or as needed.

KIDDING AND MILKING

Naturally boost your pregnant and lactating goats

RASPBERRY FOUNDATION

Grow and develop a large raspberry patch for the health of your goats!
Pregnancy Support

Ingredients

Finely chopped Raspberry Leaves

Crushed linseed

Peppermint

Thyme

Chamomile

Directions

- Store raspberry leaves in an airtight container.
- Mix equal parts of peppermint, thyme, and chamomile and store in an airtight container.
- Linseed (flaxseed): Feed at least one teaspoon per 10-pound weight for goats daily or up to 1/4 cup for goats 100 pounds or more, top dressed over feed.
- Feed your pregnant does each day:
- 2 tablespoons of finely chopped Raspberry Leaves
- 1 tablespoon of the herb mixture
- Up to 1/4 cup crushed linseed (flaxseed)

Feed fresh ivy after kidding if possible.

UP MILK PRODUCTION

Increasing milk supply naturally.

Ingredients

Fenugreek

Anise

Fennel

Borage

Directions

- Mix equal parts dried herbs in a bowl, ensuring they are well combined.
- Store the mixture in an airtight container, away from direct sunlight.
- Dose: 1-2 Tablespoons, 2x's per day.
- Or steep 1-2 tablespoons of the herbal mixture in 1 cup of hot water for 10-15 minutes.
- Allow the infusion to cool, then offer it to your goat as a natural tonic. You can mix it with their water or administer it directly.

KIDDING LIFESAVER

Use during and after a difficult birth. As written in
"The Complete Herbal Handbook for Farm and Stable".

Ingredients

8 Medium sized ivy leaves

1 Tablespoon southernwood (artemisia)

1 teaspoon chopped sage

2-3 sprigs of rosemary (1 teaspoon)

6 cloves

Directions

- Add ingredients to half a pint of cold water and slowly begin to heat to almost boiling.
- Remove from heat.
- Add a spoonful of honey and then keep covered.
- Cool and then pour off the top clear liquid.
- Give 2 tablespoons in a syringe, slowly.
- Repeat every two hours until birth is complete.
- Give the final dose as a pick-me-up.

PREGNANT ENERGY RECIPE

Use with a pregnant or with a goat who needs energy after kidding.

Ingredients

1 part molasses

2 parts karo syrup

1 part honey

*Add 30 cc CMPK to the mixture for a goat with pregnancy toxemia or ketosis.

Directions

- Blend ingredients well in a jar.
- Use a drenching gun and suck up 30 ccs of the liquid. Place at the back of tongue and feed to your sick goat.
- Repeat 3 times a day until energy and life have returned to the goat.

HARD BIRTH TONIC

When a doe has a hard birth, give them this.

Ingredients

1 spoonful of finely cut Southernwood

1 teaspoon Sage

6 spice cloves

Directions

- Add ingredients together.
- Add one cup of cold water and make a brew.
- When cool, sweeten with honey.
- Give at 2-hour intervals

AND TO THE CONTROL WE STILL HAVE!

Trust in the One who holds it all in His hands.
Psalm 24:1